Impactful Presentations
Best Practice Skills

Yvonne Farrell

MANAGEMENT
BRIEFS

Essential Insights for Busy Managers

© 2008 Yvonne Farrell
ISBN 0-9519738-7-8
ISBN 978-0-9519738-7-5

All design, art work and liaison with printers has been undertaken by
Neworld Associates, 9 Greenmount Avenue, Harold's Cross, Dublin 12.

Publisher: Managements Briefs, 30 The Palms, Clonskeagh, Dublin 14.

Acknowledgements

First, I would like to thank Frank Scott-Lennon, who provided me with the opportunity to write this book. I'm indebted to Frank for his support, advice, patience and friendship throughout the process.

I am grateful to Jane Leavy, who gave generously of her time in reading the various drafts. Jane's feedback and encouragement kept me focused.

I have really enjoyed writing this book, as it has brought back so many memories of those presentations I have given, and all those men and women who have attended my training programmes, and those I have coached. I would like to acknowledge all of them, as their learning experiences have also been mine!

Yvonne Farrell

December 2008

Foreword

Impactful Presentations provides for all the necessary direction for those who want to improve the way in which they approach and deliver presentations. The book is packed full of useful tips.

It is a very welcome addition to our developing series of Human Resource, Organisation Behaviour and General Management Books.

All of the books in the series aim to capture the essentials for busy managers; essential knowledge and skill presented in an *accessible easy-to-read style.*

A list of books already published within the series appears on the inside of the back cover; our website www.ManagementBriefs.com lists forthcoming titles.

You the reader are very important to us and we would welcome any contact from you; it will only improve our products and our connection to our reader population.

Frank Scott-Lennon
Series Editor
frank@ManagementBriefs.com

December 2008

Table of Contents

Presentations —
How we filter
information

1

Chapter outline
Presentations –
How we filter information

Introduction

In this chapter we now look at understanding the purpose and various types of presentations, and transfer of information. This is vital to making impactful, memorable presentations.

Why is it that when you attend certain presentations you come away feeling energised and enthusiastic, whilst for others you wish you had never shown up? Think about some of the best presentations you have attended. It is most likely that the presenter was the focus of your attention. It is likely that their stance, voice, eye contact, facial expressions and ability to engage with the audience were excellent, and their skill in answering questions and drawing on examples and points of information, was what you and the rest of the audience could identify with.

Many presenters make the mistake of focusing on producing slides with no consideration for the purpose of the presentation or the audience they are communicating with. Oftentimes, such presenters are seduced by their own material! As a consequence, they fail to identify with how their material should be developed to address the objective of the presentation, and the make up and expectations of their audience.

Understanding the purpose and various types of presentations and the transfer of information, is vital to making impactful, memorable presentations.

Delivering presentations is like acting and, among other things, you need to:

→ Know your script (the content)

→ Identify a process of how the information will be put across (the design and structure)

→ Recognise how your voice should sound (projection and intonation).

1.1 Purpose and types of presentations

There is often confusion with where to start when structuring a presentation. It is important to establish what you trying to achieve.

Are you trying to?

→ Sell or promote something

→ Give information or an update

→ Motivate your audience

→ Influence or positively persuade your audience

→ Provide a solution

You might argue that they are ultimately one in the same, but it is important to understand that they do vary, particularly in 'how' you put the information across. The key is transferring the knowledge you have, not in a way that suits you, but it has to suit your audience. If they can identify with the information, they are more likely to change

Panel 1.1

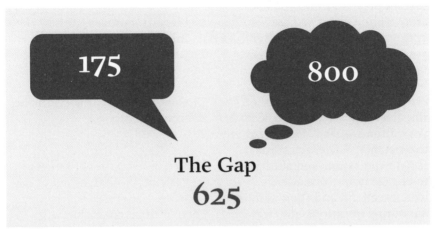

their mindset, alter their opinions, and be influenced by what you tell them. Regardless of the type of presentation, you should firstly understand how adults assimilate the information you are giving them. In the next section, we examine how the information you have to present, is transferred to your audience.

1.2 The transfer of information

You might question the relevance of considering learning theory and how the human brain works in the context of giving presentations, but understanding these helps the presenter to focus on the way their audience takes in information.

Neurologists claim that the brain, if not continually stimulated around a particular subject or task, 'switches off' every 10 minutes for a number of seconds. When giving presentations, your audience are usually in listening mode. In general, people speak at about 175 words per minute. We listen at between 600 and 800 words per minute. (Panel 1.1 above)

Therefore, if your words only develop 175 of your audience 800 thought process, then what fills the 625 gap? If all they are hearing are words, then the brain is not being fully stimulated. Their attention drifts and boredom sets in, with the likelihood of the mind drifting off onto another topic.

So how do you fill that gap?

VARIETY is the key!
Stimulating both sides of the
brain keeps your audience alert.

So what does that mean and how do you do it?

Panel 1.2

S	H	E
Sight	Hearing	Emotion

The **LEFT side** is the **LOGICAL** side of the brain and processes the factual information. It is based on rationale rather than emotion. It assimilates information through considered reasoning. We use the **LEFT** side of the brain to process information. The **RIGHT** side of the brain represents **CREATIVITY.** This is said to be where imagination and inspiration resides. By stimulating the **RIGHT** side of the brain during presentations, your audience is more likely to engage and remain alert.

So for example; when presenting your content (facts, figures etc.) you stimulate the left side of the brain, with the tone of your voice, or the colour or layout of your PowerPoint slides, or other visual aids, stimulating the right side of the brain.

When transferring information to an audience; consider some of the following:

Recall Techniques

We can recall and understand information when it is presented in a way which stimulates the three senses.

SHE represents the three senses of the brain — sight, hearing and emotion. (Panel 1.2)

→ Sight:
   We remember what we see:
   — Images
   — Logos
   — Diagrams
   — Pictures

→ Hearing:
   We remember what we hear:
   — Words
   — Music
   — Accents
   — Sounds

→ Emotion:
   We remember the feelings and emotions generated by:
   — Situations
   — Words
   — Pieces of music
   — Colours
   — Touch

So, how does this impact on your presentations? The S-Sight is what your audience sees (and that does not just mean your PowerPoint slides, but also your delivery style) and the H-Hearing, is what the audience hears (not just what you say but how you say it through projection, pronunciation and the words you use). The combination of both results in a feeling or emotion being generated in your audience, to which they will respond.

Another important factor to remember in how people recall information. If your audience can remember what your presentation is about and the key message you are trying to convey, then they are more likely to identify and respond to your presentation. It is key therefore to develop memory aids to aid in recall.

Let us look now at memory aids such as:

→ Mnemonics

→ Acronyms

→ Repetition

→ Examples

MNEMONIC:
A memory device links together two or more pieces of information to assist in recall. A **mnemonic** is often verbal and may be a very short rhyme or a word used to help a person remember something. It is based on the principle that the human brain will remember things which they can easily associate with,

is personal to them, is funny, different, or not what they were originally expecting, in other words, out of the ordinary.

Some familiar mnemonics to you might be:

❶
"Richard Of York Gave Battle In Vain" to remember the colours of the rainbow
R = Red O = Orange Y = Yellow
G = Green B = Blue I = Indigo
V = Violet

❷
Reciting the number of days in each month
"Thirty days hath September, April, June and November. All the rest have one day more, except February, one year in four, has one day more"

❸
Another mnemonic is the catchphrase
'I before E except after C', helps us remember the sequencing of vowels when spelling certain words in English. For example, in words where i and e come together, then the word is spelt in the order ie, except directly following c, when it is ei.

ACRONYM:
Using the first letter of words or phrases to create a new word which will prompt recall. The panel below shows three acronyms; each of which can

Panel 1.3

CAB	KISS	ABC
Content	Keep	Always
Audience	It	Be
Body Language	Short &	Concise
	Simple	

aid in the recall of some key considerations when making presentations. (Panel 1.3)

REPETITION:
Adults also remember information through re-capping, reviewing and repetition. Re-capping on the objectives of the presentation and reviewing the key learning points or actions required, are ways of influencing your audience. Repetition, particularly of key words or phrases, is an approach which is often used in the political and media arenas.

With the written word, repeating the same word over and over is not acceptable, but with the spoken word, the brain is more likely to recall something if it is repeated more than once. Repetition allows you to influence what is important for the audience to remember or take note of.

An example of this is the famous speech of Martin Luther King on the steps of the Lincoln Memorial, Washington, DC, on August 28, 1963.

I have a dream that one day this nation will rise up and live out the true meaning of its creed: "We hold these truths to be self-evident: that all men are created equal."

I have a dream that one day on the red hills of Georgia the sons of former slaves and the sons of former slave owners will be able to sit down together at the table of brotherhood.

I have a dream that one day, even the state of Mississippi, a state sweltering with the heat of injustice, sweltering with the heat of oppression; will be transformed into an oasis of freedom and justice.

I have a dream that my four little children will one day live in a nation where they will not be judged by the colour of their skin, but by the content of their character.

A final example of a memory aid is the use of 'examples'.

EXAMPLES:
Remember: Adults recall information when they first and foremost can identify with the subject matter and presentation objectives. Furthermore, they will remain engaged if they can associate with the examples provided. Therefore, when you are preparing your presentation, seek out examples which you know your audience can relate to.

Did you notice any acronym that could be formed from the four techniques of recall? Go back and take a look.

Yes, it is MARE

Chapter Summary

Let's jog your memory of this chapter!

→ You must always establish the purpose for your presentation

→ Ask yourself; what type of presentation is it? What am I trying to achieve?

→ Keep you audience engaged by stimulating both sides of the brain. Present the information (left brain) in a creative and energetic way (right brain)

→ Impactful presentations are about what you say (your content) and how you say it (your delivery style)

→ Your audience will remember information when you draw on the three senses of Sight — Hearing — Emotion (SHE)

→ To assist in the transfer of information you should consider the use of Mnemonics - Acronyms — Repetition - Examples — MARE

2 Key Communication Considerations

Chapter outline
Key Communication Considerations

2.1 Impact of face-to-face communication
2.2 Barriers to effective communication
2.3 Key communication considerations
for the Presenter

Introduction

A presentation is about communicating a message, and in the previous chapter, we examined how information is transferred and some memory aids to support that knowledge transfer. In this chapter, we look at the impact of face-to face communication in transferring information.

2.1 Impact of face-to-face Communication

Remember the

7%-38%-55% rule

Developed by Albert Mehrabian in 1971, when he concluded that there are three elements in face-to-face communication:

→ Words we use

→ Tone of voice

→ Body language

He also highlighted the importance of the 'non-verbal' in face-to-face communication.

This involves the communication of feelings and attitude, and tends to be demonstrated through observing the body language of the speaker.

When giving a presentation, the content is generally delivered entirely verbally, with supporting visual aids. But as a presenter, the non-verbal responses you exhibit are very important in conveying the:

→ ATTITUDE you have towards what you are saying

→ COMFORT with the subject matter or the question you have been asked

→ ENTHUSIASM for making the presentation and even towards your audience for that matter

If the words you use and the body language you display are incongruent, then your audience tends to read more from what your body language is telling them. For example;

→ **Verbally:**
"No, I do not have a problem!"

→ **Non-Verbally:**
avoiding eye-contact, having closed body language (body language is dealt with in detail in chapter 7), fidgeting, low or anxious voice etc.

If we are to relate this example to Mehrabian's findings, it is more likely that the non-verbal response of 38% tone of voice, and the 55% body language is what the audience will pick up on, more so than the 7% words they are hearing.

2.2 Barriers to effective communication

Remember, you might feel that you have all the information prepared, and that you are comfortable with your understanding of the material, but there are many barriers to communication that can distort information transfer. In this section we examine the following barriers:

→ Knowledge Levels

→ Jargon and Acronyms

→ Distractions and Discomfort

→ Language

→ Accent

→ Body Language

→ Visual Aids

Knowledge Levels

Ask yourself: how much does your audience already know about your presentation subject matter? If your presentation is too detailed, and your audience does not have sufficient basic knowledge about the subject, this will act as a barrier to the transfer of knowledge and your audience will start to switch off. Conversely, if you present the information at too basic a level, you may well activate the 'switch-off' button.

Jargon and Acronyms

Again, be aware of your audience. Are they familiar with what you are saying? If yes, do you need to use jargon or acronyms at all? Are you over using them? If you must use jargon or have developed acronyms, be sure to explain them when they arise in the presentation.

Distractions and Discomfort

Is there something that is distracting about your presentation which might take attention from you and your message?

→ Are your slides too fussy?

→ Are your slides too boring?

→ Are you, as a presenter, a distraction to your audience? That being, are your body language, your voice, or even your mannerisms taking from your message?

→ And what about the room? Is there noise outside, or constant interruptions which distract your audience?

As the presenter, you should be aware of the physical comfort of your audience. You should know:

→ How the air conditioning works

→ How to open the windows or close the blinds.

→ If your audience is too cold, or there is a lack of air in the room, or the sun is beating in on them, no matter how interesting the content of your presentation, or how engaging you are as a presenter, you will lose them if you do not manage distractions and their discomfort.

Language

If you are presenting in English, remember that it may not be the first language for all the members of your audience. Whatever language you present in, always be aware of the make-up of your audience and adapt the words you use and the speed at which you speak in order to make certain that all members of your audience can follow your presentation.

Accent

Again, as with language, be aware of your accent and how you come across. I examine the voice in chapter 7, where it is recommended that you rehearse your presentation and present on camera. Most of us dislike hearing our voice, but by reviewing the recording, you not only see your stance and body language, but you get familiar with how you sound, and over time, you will get used to hearing yourself speak. This technique is especially useful to build your confidence with making presentations.

Body Language

The 7% - 38% - 55% rule was outlined earlier in this chapter. Remember, the impact of communication is often in the body language (55%). Your body language, if not consistent with the verbal message you are conveying, will certainly act as a barrier to communication in your presentation.

Visual Aids

Be sure that your visual aids complement what you are saying. Do not have something displayed visually, whilst verbally you are referring to something else. Your audience will get confused if what they are seeing and reading is not matching the words you are saying. If your visual aids are over powering or complicated, that too will distort the flow of information.

2.3 Key communication considerations for the Presenter

When presenting you should always consider the following:

→ Knowledge of the subject matter

→ Awareness of Audience

→ Personal Delivery Skills

Panels 2.1, 2.2 and 2.3 (overleaf) develop these considerations further.

Panel 2.1

Knowledge of the subject matter

This relates to knowing your subject matter. You can not present comfortably and confidently on something you know little about.

Ask yourself:

→ Do I know enough about the subject?

→ Do I know enough to develop points of information outside of the information on the slides?

→ Do I know enough to answer questions?

If you are using someone else's presentation slides, be sure you are comfortable with your interpretation of their material, and that you are knowledgeable with regard to any references they make within the presentation.

Panel 2.2

Awareness of Audience

Again, this is key! We often approach our presentations with what we, the presenter, wants to tell our audience, with little or no thought to the experience, knowledge levels, backgrounds or status of the audience. Being acutely aware of this will have a significant impact on the way we present the information, through the examples we use and how the audience can associate with these. In the next chapter, I provide more detail on how identifying with your audience is key in structuring and delivering your presentation.

Panel 2.3

Personal Delivery Skills

These are the interpersonal skills you need to master in order to deliver confident and influencing presentations. Although these will be developed further in Chapter 7, it is key to remember at this stage that it is not just the 'what' you deliver in terms of the information, but also the 'how', in terms of your personal delivery skills, which makes for impactful presentations.

Chapter Summary

Let's jog your memory of this chapter!

→ Remember the impact your body language has in face-to-face communication. The 7%-38% - 55% rule relates to the impact of your words versus your tone of voice versus your body language

→ Barriers to communication can hinder the flow of information so always be aware of your:

- Knowledge Level
- Jargon and Acronyms
- Distractions and Discomfort
- Language
- Accent
- Body Language
- Visual Aids

→ Key communication considerations for the presenter are:

- Your level of knowledge of the subject matter
- Your awareness of your audience
- Your personal delivery skills

3

Preparing the Presentation

Chapter outline
Preparing the Presentation

3.1 Identifying and understanding your Audience

3.2 Considerations which impact on the structure
of the Presentation

Introduction

A presenter can feel comfortable with the subject matter and that they have planned what they want to say and how they want to say it — **but the most vital aspect of any communication is how it will be received by the audience.**

3.1 Identifying and understanding your Audience

The presentation must be geared, not to the speaker, but to the audience. Often when asked to make a presentation, the presenter will start by sitting at the computer typing away, producing endless slides, the content of which is from the presenter viewpoint. If you want to influence the audience, you have to do so by taking the time to identify where your audience is coming from. It is important to consider those aspects of audience interaction that are highlighted within Panel 3.1 overleaf, prior to developing the structure and writing the content of your presentation.

3.2 Considerations which impact on the structure of the Presentation

Once you have started to identify your audience under the criteria outlined above, you will write and formulate your presentation from your audience perspective. In this section we consider other aspects which will impact the structure of the presentation.

These are the 5 W's:

→ WHY?

→ WHO?

→ WHERE?

→ WHEN?

→ WHAT?

The first of these are the Why, Who, Where and When. The 5th W, the 'What', is about developing the content and structure and will be covered in chapter 4.

➡ WHY?
Why are you making this presentation? Have you identified the objectives? The starting point in planning any presentation is to identify and understand the precise objective. This should take the form of a concise statement of intent. For example, the purpose of your presentation may be to present your findings of a project, motivate your team, or even pitch for an increased budget.

➡ WHO?
Who is your audience? As highlighted in section 3.1, what are their backgrounds and experience? What are their expectations and level

Panel 3.1

Key aspects to consider about your audience

→ **Physical Characteristics:**
Consider the age bracket and gender of audience members. By considering the age group and/or gender of your audience, it can help in identifying the examples and references you provide.

→ **Educational Characteristics /Level of knowledge or skill:**
How familiar are your audience with the subject matter? Is the presentation at a level which is too basic or too advanced, based on the audience knowledge base?

→ **Occupation and Status:**
It is important to know, where possible, the occupation and status of your audience. This will help focus your mind when structuring the presentation, both at the level of detail to provide, and the delivery style and language to adopt.

→ **Type of group:**
Have they a common interest or are they a diverse group of people?

→ **Their expectations:**
Try and establish why they are attending your presentation. What have they been told about the subject matter, or you, the presenter?

→ **Their frame of mind:**
The frame of mind of your audience towards your presentation will vary depending on their business backgrounds, the timing or sensitivity of the presentation, or whether the audience has been exposed to similar content before. By identifying these prior to the presentation, you can develop your material around how, or what, the audience might be thinking, what they might already know and what they need to know.

of knowledge of the subject? Taking time to consider this will help ensure you pitch the presentation correctly with regard to the examples you use, level of detail you provide, and will influence your style of delivery.

➔ WHERE?

➔ Where is the presentation to be delivered?

➔ Are you familiar with the room layout and the equipment?

➔ Is the room comfortable and conducive to delivering a presentation?

Consideration of these factors in advance will allow you to consider how you will present. For example:

➔ Is there room to walk around?

➔ Where is the projector in relation to the laptop or other equipment?

➔ Will everyone be able to see?

➔ Is the room too bright for some of the graphics or video clips you want to show?

➔ If the room is large, will everyone be able to hear you?

➔ Will you need a microphone? If so, how comfortable are you with hearing your voice on a public address system?

If the room is unfamiliar to you, always try to have access to it in advance. Stand at the top of the room. Get a feel for the space. Know in advance where your equipment should be set up to suit you and your audience. Getting familiar with the room also helps manage nerves. There is nothing more daunting than standing at the top of an unfamiliar room for the first time, and that room filled with an audience.

➔ WHEN?

It is important to consider what day (s) the presentation will be held, and at what time of the day/evening? If presenting just after lunch, ensure that you have an interesting opening hook to grab the attention of the audience first off. Try and have some audience interaction, by asking them a question initially. Add variety to the presentation through your visual aids, using colour and/or pictures to stimulate the right hand side of the brain. Most importantly, remember to manage the tone and pitch of your voice and your body language. If your voice and body language lack energy, then your audience will lack energy and interest too.

Finally, if you are presenting at the end of the day and other presenters have run over, and, as you stand up to present, your audience could be thinking that they need to be leaving soon. Acknowledge this possibility with your audience before you start. They are more likely to listen to you if they know you are aware of the time. Adapt your presentation, telling the audience that in the interest of time management you are going to emphasise those parts of the presentation most relevant to them.

Chapter Summary

Let's jog your memory of this chapter!

→ Identify and understand your Audience before you start structuring your presentation

→ When considering your audience remember:

- Physical Characteristics
- Level of Knowledge/Skill
- Occupation and Status
- Type of group
- Their expectations
- Their frame of mind

→ Remember the 4 W's — Why (Objective), Who (Audience), Where (know your room), When (you need to consider the day and time of day of your presentation)

→ The 5th W, the What (Main Points and essential information) is covered in the next chapter

Developing the content and structure of the Presentation

4

Chapter outline
Developing the content and structure of the Presentation

4.1 What – developing the content
4.2 Beginning/Middle/End –
developing the structure

Introduction

Perhaps one of the biggest challenges in putting a presentation together is knowing what information should be included and what should not. In this chapter we examine the WHAT and follow a technique known as TRAILS to assist in this.

4.1 What — Developing the content

➔ WHAT?

What are the main points and the essential information? If you do not identify this at the start, you are likely to lose the focus of the presentation.

A key starting point when considering what information you will present is to brainstorm the presentation topic. A technique for this is to follow TRAILS.

➔ T — List all the relevant **topics** which can potentially be covered

➔ RA— Put the **related areas** together

➔ I — Compare the amount of **Information** with what you need to communicate, the requirements of your audience and time available. Be ruthless and cut back on the amount of material.

➔ LS — Develop a **logical sequence** for the remaining material

Always ask yourself: *What is my message?* **It's not so much that less is more, but that you have to do more with less.**

4.2 Beginning /Middle /End — developing the structure

The structure of your presentation should have a **Beginning, Middle** and an **End.**

The components of the **BME** model are shown opposite.

Let us now develop on the model above.

Be very familiar with the first four lines of your introduction.

Your audience will judge you from the first words you speak. Are you clear? Can they hear you? It is often during the first couple of sentences of the presentation when the presenter can feel at their most nervous. Ironically, it can be those opening sentences they often fail to prepare. So, when they first stand up to speak, they panic at hearing their own voice and realise, "what do I say as way of introduction"? Yes, they might have prepared the objective and content slide, but how do they move from those first few moments of 'the first impression', to those prepared slides?

Key to starting the presentation comfortably and confidently is to have the first introduction sentences rehearsed, but a word of warning, do not have them so learnt off that they do not sound natural!

Panel 4.2

Beginning	Middle	End
Be very familiar with the first four lines of your introduction		
Hook	Presenter Input	Review
Objectives/Content	Questions	Action Plan
Signposting	Signposting	Questions
		Hook

For example;

→ "Good afternoon!"
   I'm Yvonne Farrell of ..."

→ "I'm going to talk to you today about the art of making presentations"

→ "This presentation should last about 25 minutes and I am happy to take questions throughout"

→ "So to kick off I'd like to take you through the objective and content of today's presentation"

OR...
You could introduce your hook at this point, with the objective and content following that.

The first component in the **BME** model is the beginning.

❶ Beginning

Opening Hook − Link to Presentation /Objective - Content /Signposting

An opening hook or **link** is something at the beginning of your presentation that raises curiosity.

→ Give an example of something which relates to your presentation

→ Ask for an example of something which relates to your presentation

→ Tell a brief story which has relevance to your presentation topic

→ Cite relevant or unusual statistics in an interesting way

→ Show a visual and wait for a couple of seconds to judge reaction

→ Make a provocative statement

→ Ask your audience to think about something related to what you are presenting on

→ Ask your audience to place themselves in a hypothetical situation

→ Make reference to something that is topical in the news or within your industry

→ Ask them what do they know about...?

→ Open with a slide that has a quote relating to your topic. For example, if you are giving a presentation on managing change, you could use the following;

> *"Change is the law of life. And those who look only to the past or present are certain to miss the future."*
> - John F. Kennedy

So consider using some of the hooks outlined above to 'hook' in your audience early to the content of your presentation.

Continuing with the **BME** model, once you have developed interest in the presentation, you then outline the objectives and content.

Objectives - Content

Be sure to outline what the objective or purpose of the presentation is. Have a slide showing the content. When outlining the purpose and going through the content, be concise and to the point. Do not be tempted to go into detail at this stage, as you will ruin the structure and end up repeating yourself later in the presentation.

What relevance does this have for me? I could be out increasing sales!

REMEMBER!
There will be some who will sit in the room asking themselves, "Why am I here"? They will also be thinking about what they should and could be doing back in the office. So you have to address that question for them — What will your presentation do for them? You need to highlight the objectives and how they relate to the audience. For example; if they are sales people tell them how your presentation will help them increase sales.

Signposting

This technique outlines the presentation content at the

beginning, but ensures that the content slide is shown again at relevant points throughout the presentation.

Signposting allows you to tell your audience where you are going (a set of milestones), where you are at a particular point in the presentation and, as a way of review at the end, where you have travelled within the presentation.

❷ Middle

Presenter Input/Questions/ Signposting

Presenter Input

At this stage, you are providing the body of the presentation content. When preparing for this, it is important to consider how you are going to put the information across verbally. Where will you pause for impact, ask a question, raise or lower your voice, make eye contact etc. See chapter 7, personal delivery skills, for more detail on developing these skills.

Questions throughout

Taking questions throughout your presentation is ideal, as it not only breaks up the presentation, but questions allow you to gauge what information your audience is absorbing, and how clearly you are presenting that information.

Where time is too tight to allow questions, or if the presenter is anxious about taking questions throughout as it might throw them off their presentation, use the 'Rhetorical' question.

What is a rhetorical question and how do I use it during my presentation?

This type of question is one where an answer is not necessarily required. The presenter tends to ask it as a way of making a statement or evaluating something.

For example;
"Does this political party know how to run the country?", or "Can we change the management style of this company?"

In both cases, the question is posed, but with the effect of making a statement. By using this technique during your presentation, it gets your audience considering what the answer could be, thus moving them from a listening to thinking mode. They become more engaged and alert, as they are not sure initially, whether they will be asked for an answer or not.

Questions throughout the presentation are also useful for signposting and moving your audience onto the next section.

For example;
"Barriers to growth in the Organisation! What impact does the individual have in this?"

This question could also be shown as a slide. Not only does it act as a signpost; it can be a memory aid and signpost for the presenter.

> **Barriers to growth in the Organisation**
>
> *What impact does the individual have in this?*

Question types and handling questions are treated in more detail in chapter 8.

Signposting

As mentioned previously, depending on the length and detail of your presentation, it is good practice to show the contents slide as you finish one section and move onto the next one.

❸ End

Review and Conclusion/Action Plan/Questions/Closing hook

Review and Conclusion

Always review the main points of your presentation as way of conclusion. This can be done through:

→ Posing questions to your audience

→ Re-capping on the common threads within the presentation

→ Highlighting the key points of information

→ Showing your original objectives – contents slide

Action Plan

Be sure to outline an action plan (if there is one) again at the end of the presentation. If your audience is small enough, you should involve them in the development of the action plan, to ensure that they understand and buy in to it. Steps to develop an action plan are:

→ Establish the Critical Action Steps

→ Identify any obstacles and ways around those obstacles

→ Outline how the action plan will be implemented

→ Review what needs to be done

Questions at the end

Remember to ask for questions at the end of your presentation, particularly if time did not permit questions throughout. Some presenters are so relieved to have finished their presentation that a common mistake is to forget to ask for questions. To avoid this happening, insert a final slide with *'Any Questions?'*

Closing Hook

This should relate back to your opening hook, the opening link, which you may have used at the start of the presentation.

For example, if you are giving a presentation on managing change, and you used the following quote:

> *"Change is the law of life. And those who look only to the past or present are certain to miss the future."*
> - John F. Kennedy

Your closing hook would refer to this quotation and outline those parts of your presentation which supported the quote used.

Close Confidently

As with your opening sentences, close confidently. Do not stand there awkwardly, particularly if there are no questions or the questions have come to a natural end.

Be familiar with what you want to say by way of closing the presentation.

Examples of these might be:

→ "Well, if there are no more questions, I would like to thank you for your attention."

→ "Thank you for your attention and I wish you well in your future endeavours."

→ "Thank you for your participation today. As there are no more questions, I just want to remind you that I can be contacted on xxxxxxx should you require further detail."

Chapter Summary

**Let's jog your memory of
this chapter!**

→ To structure your information
follow **TRAILS**

→ To structure your presentation
have a Beginning - Middle — End

→ Arise curiosity and interest
in your presentation from the
beginning with an opening
'Hook'

→ Tell the audience why the
presentation is relevant to
them

→ Take the audience through the
steps of your presentation;
what you have covered, and
where you are going, through
'Signposting'

→ Be confident in the first four
lines of an introduction and
close confidently

→ Where possible create audience
interaction

→ Take questions during the
presentation, where possible,
remembering to always ask for
questions at the end

Getting your message across!

5

Chapter outline
Getting your message across!

5.1 Visual Aids
5.2 Methods to ensure variety
5.3 Room set-up and Equipment

Introduction

The focus of any professional presentation should not be on the equipment or the slickness of your visual aids. The most vital components are:

→ Your audience
→ Your material and how it impacts on them
→ The structure of the presentation
→ You as a presenter

5.1 Visual Aids

The whole idea of visual aids is to enhance your presentation, not to be the presentation itself. Too often we attend presentations where the presenter just stands and reads from boring black and white PowerPoint slides, or handouts. This is a sure way of your audience losing interest. Your audience do not want to sit listening to you read. They could do that themselves.

Remember SHE from chapter 1? We recall and understand information when it is presented in a way which stimulates the three senses of:

S   **H**   **E**
Sight   Hearing   Emotion

As the presenter, you are the principal visual for your audience. This is demonstrated through the way you stand and the facial expressions you use. You are also the voice that they hear and the conduit through which they are presented with material, to which they emotionally respond.

In this chapter, we talk about how to use visual aids and how they add to the impact in getting your message across. Remember, your visual aids should be that – VISUAL. Visual aids involve your audience, in that they are required to use two of their senses, hearing and seeing, which in turn, not only increases your audience understanding of your subject matter, but increases their retention of the information.

Studies suggest that your audience will retain (three days after the presentation) 10% of what they hear from an 'oral only' presentation, 35% from a 'visual only' presentation, and 65% from a 'combined visual and oral presentation'.

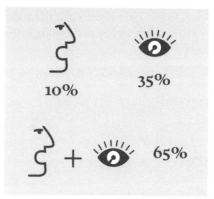

Effective use of visual aids will also assist you as a presenter. They can be a memory aid for you, and if you are nervous, using visual aids allows you to take the focus directly off you for a few moments, as your audience has to concentrate on another mode of communication.

Be clear as to why you are using visual aids.

→ Do they add to the overall message?

→ Do they reflect your message?

→ Do you really need to use them in the first place?

Often, putting more effort into the verbal aspect of your presentation can have a greater impact than non-related, or over complicated visual aids. So, the message before we start looking at the various types of visual aids is:

→ "What am I trying to achieve by using them?"

→ "Do I really need to use them at this point in my presentation?"

5.2 Methods to ensure variety

Panel 5.1

Handouts

→ Make sure they are clear and concise.

→ Provide copies of charts and diagrams (helpful if using them as part of PowerPoint presentation).

→ Can be used as a communication medium to break up a PowerPoint presentation.

→ Can be a useful way of presenting information and taking the focus off you for a while.

Posters

If the presentation has a recurring theme or a consistent message, posters could be produced in advance and are a useful visual aid.

Panel 5.2

Posters

→ Posters can be put on the wall in advance of the presentation and could be an opening hook, but be sure to refer to them early in the presentation, so that your audience is not distracted by them.

→ They can be referred to throughout the presentation and can change the medium of visual aids.

→ Make sure that they can be seen by everyone in the room.

Products/Displays

If you are talking about a product or anything that can be put on display, it can be useful to set this up in the room for use as a visual aid, or to pass around during the presentation.

Panel 5.3

Flipcharts (useful in smaller groups or where you want to gather data from the audience)

→ Check the height of the flipchart and where it is positioned in the room, making sure it is not too far back from your audience .

→ Ensure you have plenty of paper and that your markers work.

→ Stand side-on and aim to reduce the time you write with your back to the audience.

→ The flipchart is useful to record data from the group as you go along.

→ Flipcharts can be prepared in advance, particularly if you are anxious about your handwriting, or feel you might forget something when writing during your presentation.

→ You can use 'dog ear' folds at the end of the page so that you can locate the prepared page quickly and easily when needed during the presentation.

→ Enhance the visual by using colour and frames.

→ Writing should be in large BLOCK letters.

→ If you are anxious about not being able to write in a straight line, place a small dot directly across the page, where you want your words to finish. If you keep this dot in your peripheral vision as you write, directing your writing towards this dot, this should help keep your words in a straight line on the page.

→ Use a different colour to indicate the bullet point or to emphasise a key word.

→ Do not cram the page with text.

→ Invisible pencil outlines. This is where you write key information to assist your memory, in small text and in light pencil, down the side of the page. Do this in advance of your audience joining the room. When it comes to that part of the presentation where you flip over the page, all your audience sees is a blank page. You on the other hand, have light pencil outlines prompting you what you want to say.

5.3 Room set-up and Equipment

You should try, in as much as possible, to be familiar, or at least have the opportunity to see the room in which you are going to be presenting.

If you are not lucky enough to be presenting in a room which has been purpose built for holding presentations, you will have to adapt, as much as possible, your equipment and the seating layout to suit your presentation and audience.

Seating layout

Another important consideration with regard to room set-up is the layout of the room. You may not always have the opportunity to change the layout of the room you are presenting in, but do so if the need arises. Let us look now at some layout options.

Horse shoe

Panel 5.4

The Environment

→ Temperature in the room. Know how to use the air conditioning system. If your audience, or you, are uncomfortable, you should be able to identify and rectify the problem

→ Know how to open and close windows. There is nothing worse then when a member of your audience asks you to open a window and you struggle in front of your audience to do so

→ Natural light is ideal, but ensure that there are blinds on the windows in case the light shines on your presentation or in the eyes of your audience

→ Chairs. If the chairs are uncomfortable, no matter how engaging you are as a presenter, your audience will be moving and fidgeting in their seats

Positives

→ Presenter is in central position

→ Opportunity for eye contact and audience involvement

→ Audience members are not hidden from your eye contact so are unlikely to have side conversations

Consider

→ Remember to keep eye contact with those nearest the top of the room

Theatre Style

Positives

→ Presenter is in a central position

→ Good for large numbers

Consider

→ Unless each row of seating is elevated, it can be difficult for members of the audience further back to see

→ This layout is not ideal if you want to encourage interaction

Bistro Style

Positives

→ Presenter is in central position

→ Ideal for audience group work and interaction

→ Presenter can move easily around the room

Consider

→ Opportunity for eye contact

→ Difficult for audience seated at the back tables to see PowerPoint or other visual aids

Equipment – Laptop and Projector

→ If using a laptop and projector, know how they connect up to each other

→ Having an extension lead on stand-by is always a good idea, just in case the plug does not reach the socket

→ Ensure any cables are arranged under a table, or taped down with masking tape

→ What if your projector does not work or the bulb blows? Depending on the size of your audience, you can always resort to the 'Art Gallery Tour' approach.

The 'Art Gallery Tour' is a technique where the presenter always carries a colour copy of the slides. If the size of the group is less than 10 people, the presenter can hang each slide around the walls, and 'talk and walk' the group through each slide.

Equipment -
PA system - Microphone

Most people are not used to hearing their voice projected through a microphone. So, if you are using one, ensure you practice beforehand, so that you can hear what your voice sounds like.

Panel 5.5

Tips when using a microphone

→ Know how to turn the mike off and on

→ Keep the microphone at the correct distance from your mouth

→ If you are going to be moving around wear a mike attached to jacket, shirt or blouse at mid-chest level

→ If a member of your audience asks a question and they do not have access to a roving microphone, you should repeat the question so that everyone hears what was asked

In the next chapter we will consider the use of PowerPoint as a visual aid and a method of getting your message across.

Chapter Summary

Let's jog your memory of this chapter!

→ Your presentation should be a mix of both oral and visual. Studies show that an audience will retain 10% of oral only — 35% of visual only — 65% of combined oral and visual

→ Handouts are useful as they can add a different medium to the presentation

→ Handouts can be provided and referred to if an image or diagram on a PowerPoint slide is difficult to read

→ Posters can be prepared in advance, and can be hung on the wall to relay a consistent message throughout the presentation

→ Products/Displays are useful visual aids, where appropriate

→ Flipcharts can be prepared in advance and are useful to record information during the presentation

→ Be aware in advance of how the room is set up and the positioning of the equipment

→ Be aware of the seating layout. Can you influence the seating layout enhance the information transfer and your audience?

→ Know how to use your equipment

→ If you have to use a microphone, practice beforehand

Using PowerPoint for impact

Chapter outline
Using PowerPoint for impact

6.1 Designing slides
6.2 Tips for presenting with PowerPoint
6.3 Helpful hints when using PowerPoint

Introduction

Where PowerPoint presentations have become the norm, and in most cases the expectation of the audience, it has also become the style of presentation which most audiences dread to be subjected to. More often than not, presenters are found to be reading from boring slides, crammed with too much information, and illegible to the naked eye, from even a reasonable distance.

6.1 Designing slides

Where using PowerPoint, consider the following elements as covered in Panels 6.1 (below), 6.2 (right), and 6.3 (overleaf).

Panel 6.1

Slides

→ Do not cram too much information onto one slide.

→ Background of Slide. Many organisations have a house style or template. Be sure to keep slides consistent if using a house style.

→ If you do not have a house style, it is recommended to use a dark background with light text; for example, dark blue background and white or yellow text.

→ Always check how the text and background look when projected onto a screen before the presentation.

→ Bullet points should not all come up at the same time on the slide. As you are reading and elaborating on the first point, human nature being as it is, your audience will be reading down through the other bullet points. You can control the pace of information flow by having each bullet, or relevant bullet points, phased in at the same time.

→ A bullet point should be no more than one sentence across. If you must type more, 2 sentences is the limit.

→ There may be occasion where you show a slide with a mission statement or a sentence which cannot be reduced. If this is the case, highlight key words in red text or in BOLD. This will help focus your audience to the point you are trying to highlight, and it also helps you focus on what you want to say about the slide.

> **The mission of this company is to be the best in class. Research and Development is key to our success. People and their development are key to our future.**

6.2 Tips for presenting with PowerPoint

Before you start your Presentation

→ **Check for visibility from the back of the room**

Once on your feet

→ **Do not block view of projection**

→ **Avoid talking to the screen.** This is absolutely critical. Have you ever watched the person who presents the weather forecast on television? They stand almost with their back to the screen. They step to the side, glance and point at the screen, and then turn to face their audience again — practice this!

→ **Avoid reading from the screen.** Obviously the more prepared and practiced you are with the content of your slides; the less you will have to read from them. You can also show a slide and ask your audience to take a moment to read it first. That takes the focus off you and gives you a moment to compose yourself.

Panel 6.2

Font options when using PowerPoint

→ Big BOLD FONT. 36-38 point for the text of the slide with headings at least 44-48.

→ Font types such as Verdana or Tahoma are quite suitable.

→ Whichever type of font you use, be consistent. It is not recommended to be jumping from one type of font to another.

→ DO NOT USE A FULL SENTENCE IN CAPITAL LETTERS as they can be difficult to read.

→ Try to avoid red and green colours. Some people are colour blind and cannot see these colours!

→ For variation occasionally use italics and bold within the text.

49

Panel 6.3

Images for Powerpoint

→ If you include an image of bar charts, figures or flowcharts, and you have to say to your audience, "I know you can't see this..." then ask yourself, does it need to be there at all? When your audience is distracted by trying to decipher an image, they are not taking in what you are saying about it. Provide the image as a support handout if necessary.

→ There may be occasion where the presentation is going to be circulated by email, stored on a website, or shared drive and the image has to be included. In that case, for the benefit of a presentation audience, again, consider having those images as a handout.

→ Try to include images that your audience can identify with. For example; if you are giving a workplace safety presentation, take photographs of the workplace hazards with a digital camera and combine these into your presentation slides.

→ Always ask yourself when choosing an image; what am I trying to say at this point in the presentation and what does this image say to me?

→ Clipart cartoons are very recognisable and can be over familiar to most of your audience. Cartoons could end up appearing dull, or out of context with what you are trying to say. Some images might take away from the seriousness of your presentation.

6.3 Helpful hints when using PowerPoint

❶ Use the PowerPoint pen to highlight something on the screen during a presentation

There may be occasion where you might want to highlight something on your slide, underline a word, or circle something on a graph. You could insert a red box around what it is you want to highlight but another option is to:

→ Press Ctrl-P on your keyboard and use your mouse to draw where you require

→ Press the E key on your keyboard to erase the drawing

→ Press A or Ctrl-H to hide the pen once you are finished with it

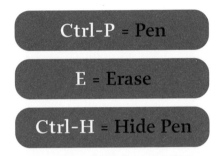

Ctrl-P = Pen

E = Erase

Ctrl-H = Hide Pen

Tip:

When using the pen, use a slow steady hand. If you are in any way nervous, it will show when using this pen function. Also, this function can look sloppy when projected onto the screen if you do not practice it.

② Moving back and forth through slides

→ There are times when you may need to move forward or back a number of slides to re-iterate your previous point or, if running out of time, skip through slides. Rather than clicking back and forth through the slides, enter the number of the slide you require on your keyboard and press ENTER.

③ Blanking the screen

→ If you want to blank the screen, either prior to or during your presentation, press B on your keyboard to blank to a black image or W to blank to a white screen. Press the same key again to restore your slide image.

All of those practices and tips in respect of PowerPoint are aimed at:

→ Ensuring that your use of PowerPoint does not obstruct, complicate or dominate your message

→ Developing your skill to a level that PowerPoint optimises your message

If you utilise the information and tips provided in this chapter then you will have mastered PowerPoint rather then it mastering you.

51

Chapter Summary

***Let's jog your memory of
this chapter!***

→ When designing PowerPoint
   slides pay attention to the
   colour of the background
   against the colour of the font

→ Your information should be
   presented in bullet points

→ Be aware of the font size
   and colour

→ Ask yourself can the audience
   read the images?

→ Are the images or cartoons
   appropriate to the message?

→ Check visibility of the slides
   from the back of the room

→ Avoid reading from the screen

→ Use the highlighting pen -
   Ctrl-P, Ctrl-E, Ctrl-H

→ Skip through slides by entering
   the slide number on keyboard
   and pressing Enter

→ Blank the screen by press B on
   the keyboard for a black screen,
   W for a white screen

→ Remember PowerPoint should
   support your message — not
   overpower it or get in the way

Personal
delivery skills

7

Chapter outline
Personal delivery skills

Introduction

Remember - you never have a second chance to make a first impression. How often have you heard that? Even before you say a word, your audience are making assumptions about you. Your presentation does not start with your first slide or sentence, but from the moment you stand up at the top of the room.

7.1 Making a first impression

If you do not have an opportunity to set up your laptop or other equipment beforehand, you will probably be required to do so in front of your waiting audience. Even at this stage, most eyes are on you. Make sure you know what you are doing, and try to appear comfortable and confident with the equipment.

→ Stance

Where and how do you stand? Be sure to stand facing your audience and stand up straight, being aware not to put your hands in your pockets, but hold them by your side and slightly away from your body. Hold your head up level, as that makes you look more confident. Make eye contact.

Talk slowly and more deliberately than you normally would. Remember back in chapter 4, we spoke about being very familiar with your initial introduction sentences. The clarity and pace of those first couple of sentences makes a major impression on your audience and their decision, at that stage, as to whether they are going to listen to you or not.

→ What to wear?

The answer to this lies in preparation, and you thinking about your audience. What type of industry or organisation are you presenting to?

What is the 'dressiquette' for them? If unsure, it is advised to overdress. It shows your audience that you have made an effort and that they are important to you. Also, even if you are over dressed, it is easier to take off a suit jacket to appear more casual than trying to dress up a pair of denims.

→ Demeanour

In making that first impression, it is important to have a warm, open facial expression. Even if you feel that it is not appropriate to smile due to the nature or content of your presentation, a warm expression, as you address your audience initially, looks far more relaxed and confident then a frown or anxious expression. If you look nervous and uncomfortable, your audience will notice that, and could start to feel uncomfortable even before you have started!

7.2 Using your Voice

Remember during the opening chapter, reference was made to the fact that delivering presentations is like acting, you need to know your script (the content), you need to know how the information will be put across (the design and structure) and you need to be very aware of your

RSVP (P)

R-Repeat   S-Speed   V-Volume   P-Pitch   (P) Pause

voice (projection and intonation). We now examine the importance of your voice in presentations. Your voice is one of the most powerful tools you have in your presentation skills tool box.

RSVP (P)

RSVP, "Répondez s'il vous plaît", is the French phrase meaning "reply, please". It has become an almost universal request for a response to invitations.

I use this acronym as a memory aid for the dimensions of the voice when making presentations, because if you want your audience to respond to you and the content of your presentation, you must develop RSVP in your voice.

R Repeat

Repeat key words, phases, or sentences *in a varied tone*.

S Speed

This signifies slowing down for emphasis and speeding up for climax or urgency.

V Volume

Always speak louder than you would if you were just sitting around a table having a conversation. Your audience has to be able to hear you at all times. You need to throw your voice to the back of the room. Project your voice louder than your normal speaking voice.

P Pitch

Similar to intonation, pitch is where your voice may rise or fall. For example, have you ever read a story to a child? You tend to raise and drop your voice to emphasise drama, humour, excitement etc. Make sure you listen to how you speak. Perhaps you could tape yourself? Be careful not to sound monotone. Think about what you want to say and how you want to say it.

> There is another P that is important for you to consider - *Pause*

Pause

This technique is where you stop for a second or two to emphasise a point you have just made, or give your audience a moment to think about something you have just said. You can also use a pause as a thinking mechanism, where you might pause to gather your thoughts, before you move on with your presentation or answer a question. Making a deliberate pause between slides, then taking a breath, can also be used to slow you down, particularly if you are nervous and are racing through the material.

7.3 Body Language

Remember back in chapter 2 when we examined the impact of communication and the 7%-38% -55% rule. This is where up to 55% of how we are communicating is reflected in our body language. Remember the example below:

→ Verbally:
   "No, I do not have a problem!"

→ Non-Verbally:
   avoiding eye-contact, having closed body language, fidgeting, low or anxious voice etc.

Here our verbal communication is telling the listener one thing, but non-verbally, our body language is telling them something else.

Body language is made up of the gestures, stance, and facial expressions you use. Body language, when matched with the message you want to deliver, helps build credibility, express your emotions, and connect with your audience. Your body language is a visual aid, which will influence your audience's level of interest and level of participation in your presentation.

Panel 7.1

Gestures

Gestures: By using your hands or head, you can support what you are saying verbally. For example; if you are talking about something moving from left to right, you can support your words with synchronized movements of your head. Or sweep the room with an open palm, as you talk about including everyone in the room in a particular initiative or project. Some people gesture almost naturally, most of us have to practice. Always be aware of your gestures. Make sure your gestures do not imply one thing, whilst you are saying something different.

Panel 7.2

Stance

Stance: How you stand tells the audience much about how you are feeling during the presentation. Stand up straight, with your weight slightly forward and your feet about a foot apart. You should move around, but avoid exaggerated or constant movement or swaying. This could be off putting to your audience.

7.4 Eye Contact

Another key skill in terms of confidence and keeping audience attention is to demonstrate confident eye contact. Your audience are more alert if they are aware of the presenter addressing them, even if it is only for 2-3 seconds. Proper eye contact helps you control the room, where your audience are less likely to drift or have off side conversations.

Panel 7.3

Facial expression

Facial expression: Move the muscles in your forehead. Now move your mouth from side to side. Move all the muscles in your face simultaneously. Why is it that when people stand up to make a presentation, their face freezes? The only movement is in their eyes. As I've just got you to experience, there a many muscles in the face. Practice your presentation in front of a mirror. Ask yourself, "if I was watching me, do I look boring or lacking enthusiasm?" Practice smiling, raising your eyebrows, raising and lowering your forehead.

Panel 7.4

Eye Contact

Eye contact: Picture a search light. Its beam of light moves at a steady pace, not too fast, but not too slowly. Now picture yourself at the top of a room, and your audience in front of you. Can you practice the same movement as a search light? Look at each member of your audience for a moment, as you move around the room.

Do not focus on just one side of the room, or just one person. This can often happen if you are nervous. Those people or that person can feel intimidated, whilst the rest of your audience do not connect with you.

59

7.5 Listening Skills

Perhaps the greatest benefit of good listening is, if you show that you are prepared to listen, your audience are likely to listen to you when you are speaking.

> "HEARING is with the ears, but LISTENING is with the mind"

Steps to active listening are:

➔ **Step**
Step way from your laptop or equipment and make eye contact with the person asking the question. This shows that you are focused on listening to them. Remember not to exclude the rest of your audience though. Once the question has been asked, you might have to repeat it to ensure everyone has heard it, but always make eye contact with everyone when answering the question.

➔ **Look**
Maintain warm eye contact at all times.

➔ **Listen**
Listen carefully to what the person is saying. You may have to answer their question with a question initially to ensure that you have the full understanding of what they are asking or saying.

➔ **Ask**
Active listening involves elaborating on a question being asked by you asking further questions to ensure understanding.

➔ **Be aware of your non-verbal listening responses**
As the person is talking, are your facial expressions and body language open and encouraging or, do you look closed, negative and intimidating?

➔ **Never have a disagreement with a member of your audience**
You may be in a situation where you have to correct something that is factually incorrect; however if the member of your audience continues to challenge you, do not enter into a full scale discussion or debate. Take it off line. Such one-to-one debate alienates the rest of your audience, who will begin to lose interest in your presentation very quickly.

Whether the audience agrees with the other person or not is irrelevant, they expect you, as the person in control of the presentation, to move the subject on.

7.6 Mannerisms

We all have mannerisms which are particular to us and are what make us individual, but they can be a distraction to the audience as well as yourself, particularly if you are nervous.

7.7 Overcoming Nerves

It is said that the fear of speaking in front of groups is one of the greatest fears people have.

Everyone has some level of nervousness, but it is how people manage themselves, how comfortable they are with making presentations, and how they channel their 'nervous energy' which makes for an effective presenter. Your audience will always make allowances for nerves, but when you do make a mistake, do not try and blunder through; stop, admit to your audience that you have lost your train of thought, that you need a moment to gather your thoughts. Relax, take a deep breath, and then move on.

Let us look now at some tips for managing nerves.

Panel 7.5

Mannerism tips

→ Remove loose change and mobile phones in pockets before you start.

→ Pens, markers and props you might use can be distracting. Put them down when you are not using them.

→ Watch that you do not wave a pointer around when you are not using it.

→ Know the layout of the room, the sockets on the floor, corners of desks etc. You do not want to fall over, or walk into them.

→ Be aware of the verbal mannerisms -'OK!' 'You know' 'Em' 'Yeah, Yeah'. These can sometimes occur when you are unsure of where you are going next in the presentation, or when you have lost your train of thought. Practice is vital here in helping overcome this. Also, once you become aware of yourself saying these, you begin to hear yourself saying it, and by practicing taking a breath before you utter it, can help eliminate the problem.

Panel 7.6

Tips to manage nerves

→ Try and be familiar with the room. Even if you have not been in the room before, take an opportunity to stand at the top, taking in the breath and depth of the room.

→ Know the equipment.

→ Remember the 2 P's, Preparation and Practice.

→ As mentioned earlier, have your introduction and closing remarks well prepared.

→ An opening hook, such as a statement, photograph or image, or asking your audience to consider a scenario, can help take the focus off you for a few moments, particularly when you are at your most nervous at the beginning of the presentation.

→ Start slowly, and concentrate on your breathing. Take deliberate breaths, more slowly and deeper than you normally would. You might feel foolish, or think that your audience can see you do this, but they can't. Training yourself to take a breath between points on your slides, or sections of your presentation, will help you to slow down.

→ A technique to take the initial spotlight off you is to start with a question. "Has anyone used this before" or "does anyone know anything about..." This is an opening hook and it gives you a moment to compose yourself whilst your audience considers the question.

→ If you feel your legs are shaking. Stand with one leg slightly in front of the other and rest your weight on the back leg. This will help ground you. Be careful not to rock back and forth by moving your weight from one leg to the other.

→ If your hands shake, do not hold them clasped at waist level for everyone to see. Hold them loosely by your side, raising them and holding your palms outwards, from time to time. This allows for some movement so that any shakes you may have are not so obvious.

Managing your nerves is about teaching your butterflies to fly in the same direction. Adrenaline manufactured by nerves can help you make strong, lively presentations.

7.8 Humour

 Jokes

The words and timing needs to be precise, otherwise the joke will fall flat. If you are nervous, it can be difficult to pull that off. Also, you might think something is funny, but your audience might totally misunderstand your humour. So, if using jokes you need to be very comfortable with the presentation, and know your audience.

→ Situational humour

This relates to humour that 'just happens' on the day. It can involve making reference to something that is happening there and then.

→ Laughing at yourself

This type of humour is where you highlight and can laugh at something you said, or did during the presentation. Most presenters do not want to appear like the clown, but having the ability to laugh at yourself shows that you do not take yourself too seriously, where it is not always necessary too.

Chapter Summary

Let's jog your memory of this chapter!

→ Making that first impression – stand tall, practice eye contact

→ What to wear? Remember the 'dressiquette' of the people you are presenting to. Dress a step above

→ Utilise projection and intonation of your voice

→ Remember - RSVP (P):

  – Repeat
  – Speed
  – Volume
  – Pitch
  – Pause

→ **Repeat** key words and phrases in varied tones

→ **Speed** up and slow down your speech to provide impact

→ Project your voice more than you would your normal speaking voice. Add **volume.**

→ **Pitch** adds variety

→ **(P) Pausing** at different stages allows for your audience to take in information. It also breaks the pace of the presentation, allowing you to slow down if you are talking to fast. Pausing can add impact if you want to put a focus on something

→ Be aware of your 'Body Language' the 'Gestures' you make, your 'Stance' and the message your 'Facial Expressions' are giving your audience

→ Eye contact and practising the search light technique is important to ensure you engage with your audience

→ Listening Skills encourages audience questions

→ Mannerisms can be part of you, but be aware of those mannerisms which distract your audience from your message

→ Overcoming Nerves by practicing some of the techniques which help those butterflies to fly in the same direction

→ Humour and jokes can fall flat if you are nervous. Situational humour can work best when the humour is in the moment and reacting to a situation

Audience Interaction – Getting them involved

Chapter outline
Audience Interaction –
Getting them involved

Introduction

Questions are an important way of introducing some audience interaction into your presentation and give you the chance to re-enforce your message. Where some presenters are anxious about taking questions, a good way to overcome this is to try and prepare for questions in advance.

But, you might ask, can you prepare for questions? You will not know what is coming, right? Wrong! You can anticipate what your audience could ask and prepare your answer. Remember we spoke in chapter 3 about identifying with your audience in advance of preparing your presentation material. Well, when it comes to anticipating questions, think about your audience in terms of:

→ How much do they know?

→ Will they understand the concepts, jargon, industry speak?

→ What are their concerns around this topic?

→ What is the make-up of the audience in terms of status, specialists and non-specialists?

Within any of the question categories above, you could ask yourself, what types of questions might they ask? You can never prepare for every question, but it is through your ability to manage and respond to questions, that your audience sees your ability to think on your feet and your level of knowledge about the subject. Where the structure and your prepared material are useful to them, questions provide the audience with the opportunity to ask what THEY REALLY WANT, AND NEED TO KNOW.

8.1 Question Types

We spoke in chapter 4 about the use of the rhetorical question, that type of question which does not necessarily require an answer, but is more of a statement by the presenter. Let us now look at other types of questions you can use to encourage audience participation.

→ **Open questions**
Which, what, why, when type of questions. "What was your experience"

→ **Specific questions**
These are used to establish the specifics or facts of a situation. The question is more direct and focused than an open question. For example; "What was your experience with the telesales system"

→ **Probing questions**
These allow you ask a series of specific questions to illicit more detail. Be careful though that it does not become an interrogation.

→ **Closed questions**
These questions require a Yes or No answer. They are useful if you want someone to be more specific or focused

→ **Hypothetical questions**
Often used in interview scenarios, these types of

questions are very useful in presentations as they place someone into a possible situation. "I'd like you to consider...", or "if you were in xxx situation, what

But, you might ask, can you prepare for questions? You will not know what is coming, right? Wrong! You can anticipate what your audience could ask and prepare your answer.

would you do". In order to answer the question, your audience has to place themselves into that scenario and consider their answer, based on their current level of information, or new information received throughout your presentation.

→ Reflective questions
This is where the presenter reflects back the question to the audience member. It can also be used to summarize the path questions are taking. Further detail on reflective question techniques will be covered in section 8.2

A key skill for any presenter is managing questions and knowing what type of question to ask - consider the 'Question Funnel'

The Question Funnel technique is useful if the presenter is trying to:

→ Delve deeper into a possible 'agenda' behind an initial question

→ Encourage the audience member to talk

→ Get clarity on what is actually being asked

Steps in the 'Question Tunnel' technique are:

→ The presenter initially asks an *open* question

→ They then try to gain more detailed information by following with a *specific* question

→ The presenter might then wait to clarify through using a *probing* question

→ Perhaps concluding with a *reflective* question where the presenter reflects a summary of the information back to the questioner

→ Finally the presenter, with the benefit of all the information gathered, answers the original question

Panel 8.1

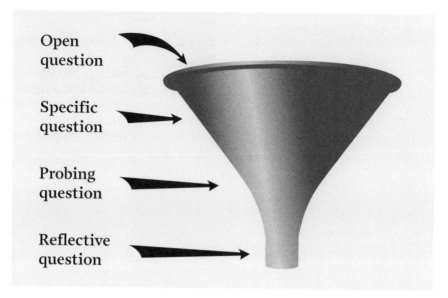

Open
question

Specific
question

Probing
question

Reflective
question

8.2 Taking Questions

When do you take questions?

You should have already considered this when you are structuring your presentation but key considerations are:

→ How much time do you have for the presentation?

→ Where do questions fit in the logical structure of your presentation?

→ How good are you with managing your time?

→ How confident are you with bringing the presentation back on track if it is side stepped by questions?

For maximum audience engagement, questions should ideally be taken throughout the presentation.

When and how do I make space for questions?

Leaving questions to the end may be the preferable option if time is tight. However, allocating time and opportunity for questions throughout the presentation helps change the dynamic. The audience moves from a listening to thinking mode. They are more drawn into what you are saying.

You might want to gauge their level of knowledge or opinion on the next topic you want to talk about. Asking them a question in advance of starting that topic allows you to determine how the audience might respond to you.

8.3 Handling Questions

First and foremost, as you practice any of the techniques outlined below, be aware of your voice and demonstrate good listening skills

Reflecting the question back to the person

This technique involves reflecting the question back to the questioner by asking, "just so that I am sure I understand your question correctly, could you give me that question again?" This will allow you time to think about the answer.

Panel 8.2

Reflecting questions back to the audience

You can do this if you are asked a question and you want to buy some time before you answer it, or again, you want to gauge the opinion of the group. It can also work in situations where you want to pull on the experience of a member or members of t he group.

→ **To the Group:**

"How does the group feel about that"?
"Has anyone else experienced/felt like that?

→ **To an Individual:**

"John, you have experience in this area!"

You have to be very confident when you get the whole audience involved and ensure that it does not escalate into everyone expressing negativity, or that the audience starts to break off into their own side conversations.

→ **Reverse back to the person who asked the question:**

"Tom, you have obviously done some thinking/have some knowledge about this — what are your ideas on it?"

Finally, if you do not know the answer to something, be honest and say so. You will lose all credibility if you try to waffle or give the wrong answer. Your audience will respect you more if you say you do not know the answer, but that you will get back to them with it.

Also by them asking the question again, in the majority of cases, the person will elaborate, as they feel that they might not have been clear the first time. These elaborations will provide you with clues as to a possible agenda behind the question.

8.4 Discussions

Opening up a discussion, either during or after your presentation, is a useful way of correcting misunderstandings. It also gets your audience engaged and allows you to measure how your presentation is going, through listening to the responses of the audience.

But remember, discussions can be time consuming and can be dominated by strong members of your audience who could end up diluting the message of your presentation – so you must be vigilant in this and manage the strong members.

8.5 Managing the 'Challenging' members of your audience

You have probably been in an audience where Mr or Mrs 'I love to talk' or the Cynic, tried to dominate the proceedings. Or what about the 'Whisperers'? Yes, we've all been there and have probably said "I'm glad I'm

Panel 8.3

Mr or Mrs 'I love to talk'

→ You can take their question or comment, thank them for their input, and move on

→ If they keep talking, focus in on a point they are making. Interrupt by saying "just on the point of… " and then once you have broken their flow, you can take back control

→ Ask them, that due to time constraints, to please hold comments and questions till the end

→ Tell them that to be fair to everyone in the audience and allow the opportunity for everyone to ask a question, please limit questions to one per person

→ If they persist to put their hand up or try and interrupt, ignore them. You are in control of the presentation. You can choose not to keep stopping to take their comment or questions

→ Do not appear rude. Acknowledge them by saying that you see they are trying to get in again, but that you will come back to them at the end or take their question off-line not that presenter, having to deal with them" or "I wish the presenter would manage the situation better"

So now it's your turn. You will find some tips for managing those challenging audience members in the following Panels, 8.3 (left), 8.4 (below) and 8.5 (overleaf).

Panel 8.4

The Cynic

→ Stay calm! You could end up alienating yourself from your entire audience if you get aggressive or negative

→ Allow them to have their say... to a certain degree, because once they have said their piece, they might just leave it at that. If you gag them immediately, they will persist throughout the presentation to be cynical and try to interrupt

→ Peer pressure. If they continue to interrupt or just loudly disagree, they are likely to offend other audience members also. By you highlighting this fact, the rest of the audience are likely to openly support you

→ There may be occasions where there is merit in what they are saying. You can acknowledge, without agreeing with them. For example; "Tom, I understand why you feel that change is bad for the company and you have been through two change programmes in your time with the company". That answer does not imply that you agree with him, it does acknowledge and validate his experience though

→ Ask the cynic to be specific. Often they will throw in a comment to distract you or the audience. If you can ask them to be more specific, to give an example of what they mean, often times, there is little or no substance to their interruptions and they back down

→ If they are taking the presentation off the point, you will have to re-state the purpose and objectives of your presentation

→ Never criticise anyone personally

Panel 8.5

The Whisperers

→ You should try and establish first off if they are lost or maybe they just missed, didn't hear, or didn't understand what you said. If they are not too much of a distraction initially, let it go!

→ Good eye contact tends to deter whisperers in your audience

→ If whispering continues, look in the direction of the whisperers and focus your voice directly at them. Not only will you be looking in their direction, but soon the rest of your audience will be looking to see what you are looking at

→ If it still continues, you can stop, look in their direction and say "I just want to ensure that everyone is clear with what I'm talking about. I'm sorry; I hope I haven't lost you both. Is there something I can clarify for you?"

Chapter Summary

Let's jog your memory of this chapter!

→ Put time into trying to anticipate the questions that might come from your audience

→ Plan when you will take questions within your presentation

→ Taking questions during the presentation, if time permits, engages the audience

→ Questions allow you to gauge how the presentation is going and audience understanding and enthusiasm for your subject

→ Remember to practice the various question types

- Open
- Specific
- Probing
- Closed
- Hypothetical
- Reflective

→ Use the 'Question Funnel' to develop the information you obtain through questions

→ Reflecting the question back to the person or another member of the audience gives you time to think about the answer. Reflecting can also be used to bring in the specialist in the audience

→ Discussions need time, but listening to the feedback that a discussion generates can allow the presenter to correct any misunderstandings within the audience

→ Manage the Challenging members of your audience — Mr or Mrs 'I love to talk' — The Cynic — The Whisperers

Notes

Notes

Notes